Animal Colours

By THOMAS FLINTHAM

SCHOLASTIC

This giraffe's a happy fellow.
He and his friends are brightest YELLOW.

The peacocks all have lots to do,
Showing off their tails so BLUE.

Flamingo friends all take a drink.
These pretty birds are tall and PINK.

Polar bear plays day and night.
His furry coat is soft and WHITE.

Raccoon friends leap and jump all day.
These cheeky pals are small and GREY.

Tiny turtles swimming in the sea,
With bold GREEN shells,
they're happy as can be.

Orang-utans swing through the trees,
With ORANGE fur and knobbly knees!

The bats just love a fruity snack,
Their wings and fur are shiny BLACK.

Snakes are in the flower bed.

These wriggly friends are brightest RED.

Butterflies are soaring high.
Bright and PURPLE in the sky.

These animals are on their way,
The Animal Party is ... today!

HOORAY!